Pragmatic Time Management Techniques

Getting things done on time, everytime!

By Damon S. Lundqvist

Damon S. Lundqvist

No part of this book may be reproduced or transmitted in any form whatsoever, electronic, or mechanical, including photocopying, recording, or by any informational storage or retrieval system without express permission from the author.

Copyright © 2014 JNR Publishing Group

ISBN-13:
978-1502307194

ISBN-10:
1502307197

CONTENTS

Pragmatic time management does not need to always consist of getting the job before you are really done doing it the right way. While this may put the problem in the "out" basket and out of your mind, it will not usually provide the best results quality wise in the end. There are various ways to get things done with excellence, on time, and still have time for you and those you love.

In the following article you will learn new skills that will show you how to not only be able to do the work before you on the day of its deadline while you maintain a work environment which is free of piled up assignments and backlogged reports. Your work life can be free of work build-up!

In the last several years we have all watched as technology skyrocketed, providing us with faster and easier ways to get things done in this high-speed world. While the software applications we utilize do have wonderful benefits, these programs seem to run us rather than the other way around. E-mail arrivals, as well as text messages and "urgent" phone calls distract us from the tasks we are trying to focus on and complete. In many ways, technology can assist us to shoot ourselves in the foot, if we let it. The following information will provide you with effective tricks, as well as some "well-kept" secrets to effective time management, and will help you to not only manage you day better, but improve your performance in the process.

Effective Secrets to Improved Time Management

You are going to learn how to take the tasks that are the most pressing demands and properly prioritize them. You will find suggestions and activities included in the contents which will educate you as to the most effective ways to get the job done when under a reasonable deadline, and get it done right. You will learn about email management, creating "closed" lists, and putting together lists of your pending responsibilities that are necessary and do-able, providing you with more structure and order when tackling you daily tasks.

The following four steps will show you how to get things done by putting them off until their time:

Make Time at the Start of the Day

This is the perfect time for you to take advantage of a bit of peace and quiet, allowing you to begin tackling the jobs that have become backed-up. You will need to prioritize these and hit them one at a time in order of importance.

Organize Your Backed-Up Tasks

Separate, classify, and place each group of tasks in appropriately marked folders. Be sure assignments are kept in order of importance.

When Urgent New Work Simply cannot be put Off…

Immediately take note (in writing) of the job that needs done. Place the reminder note where you will see it constantly, and take care of it at your earliest convenience the day it needs done.

Daily Incoming Work

Gather these things together, prioritize, and place them aside for focus the next day. This allows you to complete the plan for the here and now, and you stay steady and consistent in your completion ratio.

The above practices will inevitably assist you in forming new habits that are conducive to organization, quality production, and timely completion of tasks. Everyone from the bottom of the totem pole to the top will make great strides by implementing these suggestions and giving themselves a bit more time to regroup in their daily routine.

The Main Principles of Time Management

Having your vision in your sights

Many people possess a vision. It is vague most of the time, and typically most of these blurry visions see no honest pursuit. This is due to the obvious fact that says if the vision isn't clear, there will be no path seen in the mental realm. The path is paved with the goals which, as accomplished, bring the vision to fruition.

The vision you have must be clear. You must be aware of the particulars of each requirement that must be met, and you must be focused on diligently putting one foot in front of the other in order to accomplish each requirement successfully. To put it simply, if you want to bring your personal dream or vision to life, you must first be able to see it crisply in your mind. Bring any blurry parts into focus or eliminate them from the vision, but clear it up at all costs; when an individual possesses a vision that they can sharply perceive with their mind's eye they are also able to identify any limitations they have or obstacles they need to overcome during the dream's "gestation" period. Just keep in mind that narrowly defining your personal vision, keeping it compact and clear, will help you to keep the things before you in strong focus. Vision clarity gives you clear advice on how to act.

From a varying perspective, possessing a vision is not simply about making "to-do" lists and crossing off each item as you go. You must also take an inventory of the particular things that are not going to be pursued and accomplished. These should be listed as well, to help you make a precise differentiation between the two. There need to be boundaries set that are situation appropriate, in regard to what needs to be done. These boundaries may vary from assignment to assignment, but they will remain consistent overall.

Here is an example:

If you are shopping around for a new vehicle, you may visit many dealerships during the process. As you make your rounds, you are slowly but surely narrowing things down, whether consciously or sub-consciously, but that's what is happening. You decide against a particular make. Finally you settle on a make, but are unhappy with the dealership. You locate the right one with the right make, and you have to do a bit of talking and driving. Finally, when you have chosen you ideal new car, what you have essentially done is said "no" to every other car you looked at, in one way or another; you eliminated all the rest. This is what you need to be doing when you are prioritizing the tasks before you, regardless of the area of your life they encompass. Take what is needed and pressing. Postpone or eliminate the things that are less demanding or unneeded altogether. Now you will be able to get the real job done on time and right.

Finish Your Circles

Now that you are into the swing of "downsizing" your day, so to speak, you should notice that the list you compiled of things that needed to be done, has shrunk in size as well. They key to successful production that of which is high in quality and completed in a timely fashion, is to take a good look at that list and begin to tackle it. Start at the beginning, and only do one thing at a time. Do not proceed to the next task on the list until you have completed the first fully. There should be no loose ends of any kind in order for the task to be fully complete.

Taking on your daily responsibilities in this manner will not only allow you to dedicate yourself fully to each step of the process, but you will also be eliminating the tendency to find yourself overwhelmed with the backlog that was occurring so frequently. The end result is a great job done on time.

In reference to the "car purchase" analogy: Most of us do not anticipate buying every model of every make of automobile on the market. It just isn't realistic. Because of the cost of buying and maintaining a vehicle, we all make sure to get a good vehicle that runs great, is dependable, looks good, and is priced right. We take our time in making our decision, and we make sure we get what we want. When we look at this in reference to the jobs that sit before us and the daily routine we live out it turns out we bite off far more than we can chew. Quality suffers, deadlines get missed, stress builds, and people suffer.

In order to be a winner in the workplace you must think, plan, and carry out tasks like a success would do it. Focus on one thing at a time, and finish you circle before starting another.

A Little Bit all the Time

Studies have shown small groups of tasks, assigned on a frequent basis, promote efficient, productive thinking. This can be likened to doing your best work under pressure, perhaps, but it certainly doesn't hurt that you are ridding yourself of excess baggage and focusing on the heart of every matter before you. You are working persistently, patiently, and pounding away at each next step. This is conducive to quality, and quality prevails.

Because we are sitting down and downsizing, eliminating, and organizing our tasks and schedules, we are able to put processes together faster, which in turn enables us to do the best job possible when we begin and accomplish each task. We are able to examine and test new outlooks and ideas, and this ability gives us opportunity to be creative in our execution.

If you set a specific time to meet with your team daily for briefings, you can set a boundary regarding having to deal with related issues the rest of the day. You have dealt with that area of you job today; you will meet again tomorrow. Move to the next item scheduled, re-focus, and begin.

Clarify Your Boundaries

While all of us are frequently told to think new and objective ideas, keeping ourselves and thoughts within clearly marked limits provides us with the guidelines we need to turn out quality product. Keep in mind that taking risks in life is essential to growth and the introduction of innovative new ideas, but everything needs to have a defined space in order to provide what was asked for. New suggestions can be made after planning and determining an appropriate time and place for the presentation of the idea. Having a clearly defined set of guidelines does not limit, rather, it provides structure. There is nothing keeping you from expanding upon that structure and using your creativity to make the job within the limits even better and more compelling.

"Closed" Lists Defined & Discussed

To introduce you to the "closed list", we will define the term as a list which is complete in its entirety subsequent to completion of the last item on it. If there is nothing more to be done or added which applies to the job before you, it has been completed by means of a closed list.

One benefit of having a closed list is the fact that if any new work finds its way to your desk, it cannot be added to the closed list. You simply continue to focus your efforts on one item at a time, by order of priority, and you will successfully complete the project, and you will have completed it well.

The following is a closed list example for your reference:

Let's use the earlier scenario: Meeting with your team for briefing once daily. By implementing this method in order to deal with issues and stay on the same page you are dedicating a specific period of time toward daily team and project maintenance and improvement. You are able to face the remainder of your daily responsibilities with a head clear of anything regarding that topic.

On the other hand you could opt to deal individually with each issue as it comes up. Keep in mind that this is the best way to really grasp how much goes on during a typical workday that is a petty waste of time, and given time and space you employees will usually clear up this type of garbage on their own. When you have an "open door" policy you are inviting in every ounce of drama and criticism known to man and it continue in a constant stream throughout the day. Is the result not obvious? You are completely unable to focus on your job, your deadlines, or your other important responsibilities. It is simply ineffective and counter-productive to carry on your team meetings in this manner, wouldn't you agree?

Take the closed list method and use it in cooperation with any of the daily responsibilities you face which tend to be repetitive by nature. This will group all issues together into one space, keep order among the troops, and expose your team to daily group problem solving efforts, which is an invaluable asset to have. The icing on the proverbial cake consists of you having all the surrounding time to focus on the other priorities and responsibilities that are a necessary part of your job, and therefore, your future.

Taking the backlog problem into consideration, it is easy to see that the heart of this particular problem is working them on an open list. When a list is open-ended it takes on water like a beat-up old boat, and you will sink indeed. The solution to backlogs being eliminated is to close the situation up. If you are in a situation which is making you shake your head and wonder how to begin, implement the following:

Group the backlog into one "unit".

You need to gather the build-up together and put it in an area where it is accessible yet not blocking the way of work coming in. If you have an outrageous abundance of filing to do, and it is piled up around the office getting in the way, you need to gather it to a common area, but keep it in sight. You need to identify and solidify a solid timeframe in your schedule to get this job done, even if you chip away at the vexing backlog a bit at a time; you simply have to add it in.

Get Ready for the New Order

Since things are getting cleaned up you are going to need to change the way you have been operating things if you want the changes to last. This can be a compared closely to making a lifestyle change; old habits need to go and the holes they leave behind need to be actively filled with new ones. If any of the issues you have with time management also manifest in your day to day life, and more than likely they do, you need to begin to focus on lifestyle changes in that arena as a priority. Start small, but begin to walk the talk at home, and the work place will be a piece of cake.

You may be one who has a bit of a problem with allowing unneeded things to rent space around you. Many of you need to get serious, sit down, and begin to figure out what you have piling up that you are simply never going to refer to or need again. Time management is affected directly if you are an individual who is not managing their surroundings with order. If you resist doing this for any reason, you are more than likely not too keen on bucking up and organizing your time. This is a fact: If the person just described resembles you, and you have any desire to grow and excel in your profession, or in your life for that matter, you must begin to tend to the numerous aspects with balance and attention: individually, yet as a whole; you must also be proactive and committed if you want truly lasting results.

The Backed-Up Baggage has got to go.

The first things you need to attend to are the two steps above. When you begin to get the hang of the things discussed, and as you actively practice the methods given with dedication, this step will come naturally in a sense. While you will probably not be able to eliminate the pile or piles before you in one fell swoop, you can actively begin to take care of it daily. Start out with the things that have been waiting for attention the longest. Close your mind to any thoughts of dread or the apprehension that tends to talk you down. Grit your teeth and dig in. Schedule, schedule, schedule; close the lists you have and these things will begin to settle into a natural niche in the way you work.

Incinerate the Interruptions

Interruptions are something you have control over; you allow them or disallow them. It really is as simple as that. When you permit other individuals and the circumstances to drag you out of your "zone", you are setting yourself to have to face those piles we were discussing a minute ago. They start just that way; one interruption that leads to another, until it is common practice for you to be interrupted. Now we have negative habits forming which you alone have permitted.

We all know that things happen. We have no idea when the uncontrollable will take place, and we focus on keeping ourselves together in order to untangle the knots those surprises present. A lot of the problems we find ourselves dealing with regarding missed deadlines, overlooked or forgotten assignments, or neglected recordkeeping have to do with nothing more than disorder and lack of boundaries when it comes to the management of personal time. This is your responsibility; you alone can tailor it properly for your needs. This is one of the main reasons for touching base daily with those you supervise; now there is simply no need, short of an emergency, to bring the small, less consequential issues to you at every opportunity. If the issue cannot wait for the morning meeting, they need to get together and brainstorm with the individuals involved. If this is explained, expected, and carried by employees you have, you will not see half of the issues that take place. They will have been resolved before everyone clocked in, more than likely.

There are factors which are considered to be more random than others; random factors, as they are sometimes referred to, are more commonly known as interruptions, and they come from just about every individual, situation, and direction you could possibly imagine. Some of the "random factors" which tend to pop up throughout your typical day may include interactions with your supervisor, telephone calls or pop-in meetings with customers and/or clients, emergencies in our personal lives, and countless others. While there are some that are genuinely uncontrollable and must be dealt with by deviating from the schedule and plans you have made, there are those which only continue because you have permitted them to do so. A family emergency is far different than a teenage daughter calling to complain that her brother ate her cold pizza. Make your personal boundaries clear and concise if you genuinely want to implement improved time management into your life. You can continue to do things on an 80 20 basis, but you will simply fall behind, burn out, and eventually grieve the lost time and opportunities that have been missed. You can indeed dodge this bullet, and dodge it easily.

Remember, once you have set your personal priorities and scheduled them accordingly, and once you have set you boundaries and made your limitations known to all concerned parties, it is time for you to take over. Now you must sit down and focus on holding yourself accountable to follow through on the schedule you have set by tackling the work before you.

Novelty or Just Devotion?

You may have watched a mandatory video at work, or perhaps you read a magazine article in the waiting room at your doctor's office, which talked about effective time management skills. Perhaps this article was so compelling you developed a deep interest in finding out more about some of the things you may have been doing wrong and how you could possibly change them up. Having an avid interest is a great start, but to make a change as profound as the one we are discussing involves commitment and devotion. Making a change in lifestyle is about changing damaging habits into healthy and productive ones, and learning to implement proper time management is no different.

If you are dedicated to making a serious change in the way you have been doing things at the work place, you must also be dedicated to making some changes at home. True, productive routine that is holistically healthy does not begin at 9 a.m. and end at 5 in the afternoon. It is something that must be practiced with consistence and with dedication if results are to be seen, and the practice must continue to be lived out if you want the results to be of lasting benefit to yourself and those around you.

Evaluate where your commitments lie before you begin. Take a good hard look at whether or not your priorities have been out of whack, or if they just need a bit of rearranging. Use the knowledge you gain when you do this project to be your guide in making a firm decision to act. Are you simply attracted by the novelty of change? Do you think you will bore easily when change does not happen overnight? Maybe you are willing to do what it takes and patiently endure. Are you willing to commit? Ask yourself these questions before making your personal decision.

If you are not committed to any undertaking which you are considering, you have absolutely nothing to motivate you. When you make a commitment, it stems from a passion which has developed for the object of your consideration, and it is this passion which solidifies your desire to commit. Without this passion, the things you get excited about will be few, far between, and the commission will be short lived. A choice needs to be made between being immediately satisfied and coming up short, or working hard, practicing patience and diligence, and reaping the benefits in the long run.

So what do I Need to Do?

Now that you have read the seven techniques mentioned above, and now that you have had some time to process the information given to you regarding each, it is the perfect time to take the following into consideration:

Is it really possible to for me to implement change into the random nature of my day to day life?

Do you believe you can accomplish this goal, or any goal for that matter? You must establish trust in your abilities and the level of dedication you are investing.

Can I utilize the techniques I have learned in a manner that is organized and effective?

The methods described have been given in a particular order for a reason. Begin your new practices right here and now by taking these techniques and applying them to your personal commission of them. It is a perfect opportunity to break in your new "shoes".

Creativity in Organization as it Relates to Effectiveness

Having all your eggs in one basket simply consists of managing an orderly, disciplined life, and this is something that you alone carry out for yourself. You can have creativity up to your eyeballs, but if you're the surrounding portions of your life are in chaos you will be ineffective to a degree. We can safely look at levels of effectiveness as direct reflections of the order we possess and maintain in our work and personal lives; the two walk hand in hand. Organization, when married together with creativity, produces a high level of effect.

Another excellent point to keep in mind is the fact that "activity", in itself, is not in the same category as "action". The two terms are easy to confuse, for example, just because you are running around like a chicken with your head cut off doesn't mean you are getting anything done.

If you have been living a life filled with difficulty in regard to the level of organization and time management you are lacking, do not despair. A restructure of your daily routine and some changes in your personal boundaries in specific areas will make all the difference in the world. If you make a firm commitment and live it out, it will change you career and your life.

It is vital that you develop a clear knowledge and vision of what you desire to become and to have. You must then sit down and patiently put together an appropriate strategy to obtain your goal which suits your situation and potential obstacles. By following this plan of attack you will remain focused, and your determination will push you in the direction you need to go to begin to effectively manage both your time and your life.

If we, as human beings, had complete control over the numerous aspects of our lives, the following would be possible:

They would be potently self-motivated.
Ripping through an entire day's reports would be nothing.

They would get everything done, every day.
You would find we even had time left over to go out with the boys before going home for family game night.

They could accomplish the tasks neglected by others.
The guy next to us would have his job in a complete jumble. Ours would be great, and we could clean his up, too.

They know there stuff beforehand.
A hard look has been taken at what needs to be done ahead of time. It is planned out, and by the next day, you already know when your tasks will be completed and done well.

If they hit a bump, they figure it out and don't hit it again.
If, for any reason, the planned agenda you have created falls apart, you will be active in sitting down and figuring out the direct area of trouble. If it can be fixed with an adjustment, you follow through accordingly.

Delegate, but don't tempt fate.
While you pass on levels of authority, you would never let the authority you have delegated go unsupervised by you, and you are strategic and

discreet in your methods.

Future dreams would finally enter the planning stage.
You would sit down, at last, and begin to implement, into your schedule, the beginning steps you need to take in order to achieve your lifelong dream.

They would be fast in their efficient productivity.
Not only are you getting things with excellence, you are getting it done consistently fast.

Emergencies don't Even Phase Them.
It doesn't matter what kind of situation arises. If you are an effective manager of your life's various aspects, you will know what to do and when to do it. Panic will be far from you; you are adapted to keeping your thoughts focused on taking the next right step.

They would possess the skill and ability to take on more.
Even if you have a few morsels remaining on your plate, your high level of organizational and time management ability would enable you to assist others in their quest for project completion. Share your secrets with them if they seem to need the changes you are making.

Press On

Now you have you plan and you have begun to implement the principle you have learned. You are moving right along. What are the things you can do to maintain the ground you have gained while continuing to make strides? How can you avoid stagnation and complacency? If you want to get rid of the habit of putting things off, and you want the habit gone for good, below are some great suggestions that will help you make some changes. Consider and practice the following:

Rolling with the Flow Once Again

Conduct a private, personal inventory consisting of the following:

Have I given myself a sufficient amount of time for the task?
Am I working in a manner that is productive and efficient?
Have I overloaded myself with too much work?

Make a "Determined-to-do List"

Once you have this list down on paper, the next steps are to prioritize, organize, and act, act, act!

If you are getting Behind, Dam up the Backlog Leak

At the first tug you feel to your gut that you are getting overwhelmed, the proverbial foot needs to go down immediately. This will be the wisest and most productive action you can take, and you would do so promptly.

Do it Until it's Done

Make your plan and execute it. You must set your focus and keep it.

Dealing With "Reaction"? Fake 'em out!

Take on the pretense that you are going to do absolutely nothing at all.

Tell yourself that the action you're going to proceed with is going to be completely painless in nature.

Work in Set Groups of Time

When working, set a timer or an alarm to sound after a short, pre-determined amount of time; during that time fix your focus firmly on the task before you. Make your limits clearly known beforehand regarding interruptions and your expectations regarding them.

How are you feeling?

Keep an attentive mind in regard to your emotions. Are you feeling good in general? What are you emotions like most of the time while carrying out your daily tasks? If necessary, write down in a journal the information you observe. Use this information for comparisons after a week, two weeks, or even a month. It will help you to identify triggers and patterns, which will enable you to be proactive in resolving the issue.

Allow Yourself to Rest

It is imperative to your ability to apply your skills, reason, and deliver quality work in a productive fashion, to schedule regular times for rest and play. Without this type of activity regularly introduced into your schedule, burn-out is inevitable. You will find yourself sliding backward, losing ground in regard to the gains you have made. At that point you must turn around and identify the point of err, which will in turn enable you to rectify the situation.

Effective, high-quality careers and lives are lived by those who have highly organized and prioritized lifestyles. Choosing the battles you are going to fight is a necessary part of success, and time management is the very essence of that art. It is an assertion of what you are claiming for the day ahead which you need to live. It is a statement of your expectations and boundaries, and it is a statement of your commitment to your job and your life.

Sit down today and consider the state of your personal and professional affairs. Make a quality decision in accordance with the things you desire to change, and commit to make these changes in all of your life's aspects. If you reflect on this day and the state your life is in now, and you compare it to the life you are living after 5 years of consistent practice of these principles, you will see a life unrecognizable. Decide and act today!

If you liked this book, please consider leaving a positive review so that other's may gain the same insights and knowledge that could also help them!

I do not have an advertising budget, so support in the form of positive word of mouth from people like you would be immensely appreciated!

Thank you for buying this book and till the next time! ☺

Damon S. Lundqvist

This guide is not intended as and may not be construed as an alternative to or a substitute for professional business, mental counseling, therapy or medical services and advice.

The authors, publishers, and distributors of this guide have made every effort to ensure the validity, accuracy, and timely nature of the information presented here. However, no guarantee is made, neither direct nor implied, that the information in this guide or the techniques described herein are suitable for or applicable to any given individual person or group of persons, nor that any specific result will be achieved. The authors, publishers, and distributors of this guide will be held harmless and without fault in all situations and causes arising from the use of this information by any person, with or without professional medical supervision. The information contained in this book is for informational and entertainment purposes only. It not intended as a professional advice or a recommendation to act.

Other books by JNR Publishing Group

The Seduction Force Multiplier 1- Bring Out Your FULL Seduction powers through the Power of Routines, Drills, Scripting and Protocols

The Seduction Force Multiplier 2 - Scripts and Routines Book

Damon S. Lundqvist

The Seduction Force Multiplier 3- PUA Routines Memory Transplant Package

The Seduction Force Multiplier 4 - Situational PUA Scripts and Routines

The Seduction Force Multiplier V - Target Auto Response Package

The Seduction Force Multiplier VI - PUA Innergame, Mindsets and Attitudes

Shielded Heart - How To Stop Yourself From Falling For A Seduction Target

Damon S. Lundqvist

How To Cheat Proof Your Relationships

Secrets to Hacking Your Brain- Be Your Own Therapist

28

Hypno Machines - How To Convert Every Object In Your Environment As a Device For Psychological and Emotional Manipulator

The Art Of Virtual Practice 2 - Learning and Mastery Of Any Skill At Lighting Speeds!

How to Operate with Your Full Potential and Talents

Damon S. Lundqvist

<u>*How To Master Resilience And Be Invincible To Life's*</u>
<u>*Disappointments And Failures*</u>

<u>*The X-Factor Manual*</u> **- *Learn How To be A Model Even If You Don't Look Like One***

The Age Erase System - Hypnotic Anti Aging Serum

Develop Insane Self Confidence and Naturally Unleash The Supermodel Within

The Persuaders Guide To Eliminating Resistance And Getting Compliance

Damon S. Lundqvist

The Art of Invisible Compliance - How To Make People Do What You Want Effortlessly

Unstoppable and Fearless - Know What You Want and Get It

Just Go- Having The Courage and Will to Pursue Your Dreams

How To Make Better Life Decisions

How To Diet Like a Machine- Make Any Diet Program Work With Ease

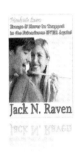

Friends into Lovers: Escape and Never be Trapped In The Friendzone Ever Again!

The Permanent Anti-jealousy Solution

The TEN Game Operations Manual: How To Get Extremely Gorgeous 10s Consistently and Predictably!

How Not To Give a Shit!: The Art of Not Caring

Damon S. Lundqvist

Perfecting Your Game: How To Reach Mastery Through Perfection Of Game!

Manipulative Eye Contact Techniques: Install thoughts and feelings just with your eyes!

The Injector Protocol: How To Inject Your Essence Literally Into Everything!

Hyper Learning Techniques: How To Learn at Super Speeds!

The Anti-AA Eradication System : 100% Foolproof Approach Anxiety Elimination Techniques and

Protocols To Enable You To Start Approaching Dozens of Women Today!

The Ultimate Dog Training Crash Course

Maximized Energy = Maximized Potential: How to pursue the most difficult tasks with your maximum energies and potential!

!

<u>*Tough Love: Surviving and Winning The Most Difficult*</u>
<u>*Romance Games, Relationships and Lovers From Hell!*</u>

<u>*Acting and Comedy Techniques for Seducers and PUAs*</u>

Putting Mind Control In Your Daily Life

Seducing the UNseduceable Man: Specialized seduction techniques for the impossible to get man!

Be A Human Lie Detector: Detect High-Level, Covert
Communications of Persuaders, Seducers and Other
Manipulators!

2- Styles of Communications:Perfectly calibrated
communications everytime!

Techniques on Developing Irresistible Charisma at Work: A tactical-manual on how to be the ultimate People-person everyone likes and follows!

The Ultimate Guide On Manufacturing REAL Luck

Proven Strategies To Taking Control Of Your Life By Creating Your Own Luck!

Imitate, Innovate and Annihilate! How to Clone And Improve On competitors' Best Products and Services Effectively!

How To Increase Reputation and Popularity! Applying Practical Brand Management Principles For Businesses and Individuals

The Ultimate Business Competition Guide: Reverse Engineer The competition and Make 'em eat your dust!

How to Achieve Mental Mastery by Maximizing Your Brain Performance!

Reach Your Full Brain Potential by Adopting Proven Thinking Methods to Drastically improve Your Mental Skills, Discipline and Development

Develop Irresistible Skills of Persuasion, Motivation and Leadership at Work And With Friends!

Learn the fine art and science of persuasion and motivation to effectively influence people...

.

The Ultimate Guide On How to Be Naturally Persuasive

Influence People Without Manipulative Persuasion Tactics and Strategies

Develop Powerful Business Thinking and Reasoning Processes

How to choose the PERFECT thinking styles to think smarter, better, clearer for any situation!

The Ultimate Guide to Developing a High Performance Mentality

How to achieve anything you want by thinking like an Overachiever!

The Ultimate Guide to Counselling, Coaching and Mentoring

The Handbook of Coaching Skills and Tools to Improve Results and Performance Of your Team!

The Ultimate Guide on Developing Conflict Resolution Techniques for Workplace Conflicts

How to develop workplace positivity, morale, communications.

<u>*The Ultimate Guide on Proven Communication Techniques and Presentation Secrets*</u>

How to Communicate with Power and Improve Your Persuasion IQ at Work and in Everyday Life!

<u>The Corporate Warriors Manual</u>

Applying Military Principles to Conquer Business and Life!

<u>The Ultimate Burnout Cure</u>

Re-ignite your passions in life and work!

<u>The Winner's Code</u>

How to unleash the winner within

Maximizing Results Through Minimalism

Get the most out of life by focusing only on the essentials!

The Ultimate Guide To Executing Strategies, Plans & Tactics

Practicing the Art of Execution

The Ultimate Collaboration & Synergy Guide

How to bring out the best performance and results from everyone!

Being the Action-Man in Business

How to start making things happen today!

Hit the Ground Running in Business

Learn Must-know Business Fundamentals for the New Entrepreneur

Conflicting Views

Tactfully handle any conflicts in any organization

The Ultimate Guide on Developing Patience

Be a better leader by expanding your patience!

Damon S. Lundqvist

Designing & Projecting Powerful First Impressions

Pragmatic Time Management Techniques

Getting things done on time, everytime!

The Fine Art of Decision Making

Make things happen by making the right calls!

The Ultimate Guide to Building & Managing the Perfect Team

Parenting and Disciplining Strong-Willed Children

Advanced parenting techniques for defiant children!

Advanced Parenting Techniques of Rebellious Teens

The ultimate guide to parenting difficult teens from hell!

The E.Q. Genius

Mastering Emotional Intelligence

The Ultimate Guide to the Placebo Effect

Understanding and exploiting Placebo effects in health & life!

Mastering Creativity and Inspiration

Cures to your Creativity Problems Revealed!

The Ultimate Guide to Developing Belief in Yourself

The Inner and Outer Games of Developing Trust and Belief in your Capabilities!

Bonus!

Sample Chapters of the book:

Manipulative Eye Contact Techniques:

Install thoughts and feelings just with your eyes!

Jack N. Raven

Punishments

Do the exact opposite of what I said in the previous section. You can show the opposite of fascination, which is showing signs of boredom. You can roll your eyes or create the expression that you are about to fall asleep. You could also look fierce or hostile towards her. You can just antagonize her with looks alone. You can even look at her head to toe, and many other things—just use your imagination.

By pretending the person doesn't exist, like how we see vagabonds and peddlers on the street-we invalidate their existence!

The eye communications to punish should not be accidental. The person has to FEEL your message.

Indicators of Interest

Indicators of interest (or IOI's) are used in the seduction community to determine whether a target is showing signs of attraction, or that you need more work to get her attracted. The most obvious signals could be that she's looking at you like you are the most interesting person there. She's looking at your chest; she gives you that puppy-dog look that she's almost mesmerized by you. When you're talking, 100 percent of her attention is on you!

There are some not so obvious signals that may require a little bit of decoding. Both indicators of interest, and opposite, which is "IOD", or indicators of disinterests are all important to read. We'll get to that in a little bit.

Using the same metrics from earlier, you can tell a lot by the direction she's looking at, the intensity, and many other things. Women are actually better at this—sending and receiving nonverbal communications. The average guy has no idea what's going on—we have to be taught these skills.

These things come naturally for women, they are hardwired to be sensitive to these invisible messages because they are keenly aware of this channel of communication, you can now use this to send out the desired messages. If you're going to use this to flirt, the same indicators of interest and disinterest can be calibrated accordingly to send the appropriate message that you want. As she is talking, if you want to sub-communicate that you actually appreciate her more than for her looks, instead of looking at her boobs or ass, you can just be looking at her face where her eyes are!

If she just bought this bracelet and you just noticed her eyes looking at it trying to direct attention to it? She would appreciate it if you would pay attention to the bracelet and how great it looks on her!

A woman just gives out signals on the things that she wants to be appreciated for, and you can use your eyes along with your words to compliment. Some women from time to time need their ego stroked. You can easily do this with no effort just by looking at their faces and appreciating their beauty. A woman just likes to be thought of as beautiful; even those who get looked a lot. They can still appreciate that nonverbal compliment of just being stared at, and nonverbally told how gorgeous they are.

You can appreciate non-physical traits through your eyes. For example, if she sings well, she might think, "Are your eyes showing appreciation?" Well, you can just mentally focus and sub-communicate that you are appreciating the music and look like you are mesmerized by her voice.

You can look at any one specific thing exactly, but overall, it can easily be communicated, and she'll fully get it! Understand how subtexts work and all this becomes a piece of cake!

If the target is a chef, how would you compliment her cooking with only your eyes? Simple! Look at the food she's prepared, and how a five-year-old fat kid looks at an ice cream truck! Like he can't wait to eat it. Almost like it's the most beautiful thing he's ever seen in his entire life! Then, when you actually put it in your mouth, you are intoxicated, like you are in heaven or something. If you're there during the preparation, you can also show appreciation by how impressed you are how meticulous, professional and talented she is.

No words needed to be spoken at all.

The problem with over-complimenting is that you could

come off weak, trying to impress her: being a kiss-ass! You don't have be that transparent. Compliments can be relayed without words!

How to show fascination with the eyes

By the same principles of subtext again, you can just look into her eyes and mentally go through a list of the things you appreciate about her. It does not have to be real because you can use anything real or imagined. Let this be real in your mind—whether made up or not—like you have to be going soon, as you're looking at her! For example, you can say in your mind how you like her for being that one in a million chick or that she's smart (even if she's not) or that she is a good dancer or whatever it is that you truly like. Make believe that she has it and appreciate it one by one as you're looking into her eyes. Make believe that these traits belong to her! She will just get that message somehow. She'll understand it and receive it as a compliment although you haven't said anything! It doesn't lower your value at all.

Eye communications for instant isolation

When you get the target engaged and when you're looking eye to eye lost in each other's gazes, it's like the world disappears and only you and this person exists. That is kind of effect we want! To isolate or be with the target with you in private without moving anywhere!

Mentally once a target is engaged completely it generates the same effect, though in reality she hasn't moved.

The more common way to isolate is physically move a target away from her friends. That's still necessary for some many isolation needs, but in other situations we only need to immerse and get the target engaged by creating that virtual couples bubble that only the two of you live in.

To do this, there must be a reason why both you are looking at each other intently in that way. It normally happens in normal interactions between people talking about a topic that deeply engages them.

So one way to go about this is to come up with highly engaging material or topic, they have no choice but to be fully immersed in the experience in this moment!

You can do so much and say so much with your eyes alone! Knowing the technology you can also transmit the same verbally and nonverbally with your other senses.

Occasionally the friends might be alarmed by the level of engagement of their friend. So they try to run confusion by breaking her state. Once the state interrupt happens, and you haven't done enough work? That may be the end of it! State interrupt happens when you are in a state of trance that you're mesmerized and deeply entrained so the friend(s) try to interrupt that deep engagement by changing topics, pulling her away to dance, asking a dumb question etc.

Making subtexts real

How do you make subtext real? You make it real to the observers by first making it feel real inside of you! You have to feel the sensations, actually see and hear the experiences on the inside for others to be convinced. You can make that special look that you've met someone before, and this accidental meeting is actually the second meeting. She will get it! She might actually be persuaded to believe that you've met before, even though you really haven't. This works because it is open-ended as long as she can be 100 percent sure you haven't met, and that there is a possibility that you have.

This is so accurate that those doing surveillance on targets, even if they are using or wearing misleading uniforms, they can tell ranks, just based on the eye contact. Who's calling the shots, and who is following. Though they may try to play the role of being the inferior, eye contact alone can determine who is who in the pecking order.

You cannot convince others if you are not convinced yourself. Not only must you be convinced, you must be absolutely flawless in your beliefs. There must not be any holes because you use the indomitable belief to out-frame the other person.

Any hesitations or insecurities? Expect other people to sense it! Make it strong and unbreakable? It can shatter the foundation of their beliefs!

Be a hundred percent absolutely sure whether it is real or not is irrelevant. You just have to believe it as if it were real!

That was just an example of the many things you can do with this ability. Just copy how people look at different people or the relationships in their lives. A subordinate looks at her boss differently from how she would look at a peer, close friend, a lover, etc. There are patterns that you need to observe closely, then list them down and get the exact physicality (how something looks physically). Once you do this, you can copy them exactly and generate great results-maybe even identical results if you do it properly.

Printed in Great Britain
by Amazon

69495277R00038